EDOUARD MANET

T&J

Published by TAJ Books International LLC 2013
219 Great Lake Drive
Cary, North Carolina, USA
27519

www.tajbooks.com
www.tajminibooks.com

ISBN 978-1-84406-251-5

Printed in China

1 2 3 4 5 17 16 15 14 13

EDOUARD MANET

T&J

BY SANDRA FORTY

EDOUARD MANET

1832–1883

Many art historians believe Edouard Manet is the father of modern art. Although often cited alongside the Impressionists, he was not a member of their group and never exhibited in their Salon des Réfusées. Instead, he pioneered a path between realism and impressionism, choosing contemporary subjects and composing them in a truly modern fashion. By doing so he became a controversial painter, offending critics who considered that art should follow the traditional established precepts of technique, subject, and composition, and being applauded by the (generally) younger audience who was excited by his new vision and approach to the medium.

Many of Manet's paintings provoked outrage and scandal but his most controversial work was *Le Déjeuner sur l'Herbe* (*Luncheon on the Grass*), which showed a naked woman enjoying a picnic beside two fully and conventionally, if rather exotically, dressed men. Today it is hard to appreciate the shock it caused, but at the time the painting became a real cause célèbre.

Manet was particularly inspired by the Spanish realism of Velázquez, who he idolized and called "the painter of painters," and other 17th century artists such as Bartolomé Murillo. He particularly admired the way they showed ordinary street people and the poor urban workers of the slums and back streets without exhibiting judgment or romance about their subjects' circumstances. Consequently, about half of his output was scenes of his fellow Parisians going about their daily lives in the city. His early style was influenced by the realism of Gustave Courbet's loose brush strokes and simplified details. While he was learning his trade he painted the usual topics of mythological, historical, and religious subjects but after he developed his own style he rarely returned to such conventional ideas.

Manet became one of the first artists to make the common man (and woman) the theme of his work. His preferred subjects were compositions of people enjoying their leisure time in the parks, cafés, and amusement centers around Paris. He also liked his subjects dressed in unexpected outfits, a quirk that many observers found distinctly peculiar. The Impressionists, with whom he became close friends, found his work inspiring and continually tried to get him to exhibit alongside them at their exhibitions but he never did. Like many of his contemporaries, Manet was influenced by the major Japanese artists of the day and the unusual compositions and use of flat color of their woodblock prints.

Manet lived and worked at a very exciting time in terms of politics and art. He counted many of the great names of French late-19th-century culture among his friends, many of whom—such

Self-portrait with a palette, 1879

as Stéphane Mallarmé, Antonin Proust, and Emile Zola–he painted. Portraits of his family and friends were also numerous among his works.

The Paris Salon was the arbiter of acceptable art. The Salon hung an annual government-sponsored exhibition of contemporary paintings chosen by a jury of wealthy and influential art critics who decided what was good enough for exhibition and rejected the rest. Their taste was alarmingly conventional and they were heavily resistant to modernism and change. Manet ached to be acknowledged as a great artist, but to do so he had to be accepted by the entrenched art establishment. Nevertheless, he insisted on being taken on his own terms, not theirs, and waged a career-long battle with the Salon. By the end of his career, he had mixed success. The Salon accepted some paintings and rejected others, but he was determined to prevail and although occasionally discouraged was persistent in his attempts to get his works hung in the annual exhibit. Manet said, "The attacks of which I have been the object have broken the spring of life in me ... people don't realize what it feels like to be constantly insulted."

One of Manet's pioneering techniques is called *alla prima* in which he placed the color he wanted directly onto the canvas instead of building up layers of tints. This technique was particularly effective when painting *en plein air* and trying to capture a fleeting sunlit scene or light effect. His approach to painting was taken up by the Impressionists, for whom he became rather a hero. The Impressionists too were trying to capture the passing, fleeting moment in a flurry of quick brush strokes. Similarly, many of Manet's works are almost photographic in their composition and use of light. As a result, these works had a distinctly modern look for that time, which unnerved critics and alarmed contemporary audiences but inspired the admiration of young, upcoming artists.

Manet, however, preferred working in his studio to being outside. His works are characterized by their solid construction and unorthodox, flat schemes of clear color. A frequent comment about his paintings was that they were too sketchy, showing a loose technique that was thought to lack academic rigor and which many described as crude. As he said, "There are no lines in nature, only areas of color, one against another." Unlike the Impressionists, he made frequent and deliberate use of black and other dark pigments. He is said to have remarked "black is not a color," yet for his purposes he used it liberally and dramatically.

Compositionally Manet did not reject the historical traditions of his predecessors, but instead updated them with contemporary realities. Despite the comfort of his relative wealth, Manet was still eager to achieve acceptance as an artist and would drop into bouts of depression when his paintings were harshly criticized. In January 1865 he became so dispirited that he even destroyed a couple of his paintings.

Edouard Manet was born on January 23, 1832, at 5 rue des Petits-Augustins, Paris, into an affluent and politically well-connected family. His father, Auguste Manet, was a French judge who confidently expected his son to follow him into the law. His mother, Eugénie-Desirée Fournier, was the daughter of a Swedish diplomat and the goddaughter of crown prince Charles Bernadotte of Sweden. They had two more sons, Eugène and Gustave.

During his conventional education the young Manet was frequently taken to the Louvre by his maternal uncle, Edmond Fournier, who enjoyed his nephew's interest in art. In 1845 Uncle Edmond encouraged his nephew Edouard to enroll in a dedicated drawing class at the Collège Rollin to refine his technique. While there Manet met his lifelong friend, Antonin Proust, who in time became a respected journalist and politician as well as the French Minister of Fine Arts.

From an early age, Manet was much more passionate about art than his school studies, but to please his father at the age of 16 he agreed to apply to attend the Naval Academy. When he failed the entrance exam he joined the cargo ship Havre et Guadeloupe as a student pilot and sailed to Rio de Janeiro in 1849. The appointment was entirely designed to teach affluent young men how to pass the Academy exams and was not an arduous job. Manet frequently wrote home and in one letter to Eugène said, "I don't expect to pass the exam this year. There are even more distractions on board a ship than there are on land." He predicted correctly and failed a second time a few years later.

Before he left for the high seas, Manet started an affair with the family piano teacher, Suzanne Leenhoff, that resulted in the birth of Léon-Edouard Koëlla on January 29, 1852. To avoid a scandal, the baby was passed off as Suzanne's younger brother and Manet became his godfather. Leon was to become a frequent model for his "uncle" and is featured in a number of his paintings. Leon was 18 before he was told of his true paternity, if he was ever told at all. Manet's father was probably never told about the baby as the scandal would have deeply shocked him and disgraced the entire family if it became public knowledge.

After a year at sea Manet returned with a portfolio full of drawings and paintings that he showed to his still unconvinced father, who finally agreed to allow him to attend formal art lessons. Manet, however, was not prepared to attend the conventional École des Beaux-Arts where he would be taught the classical artistic disciplines. Instead, he chose to become the pupil of Thomas Couture at his independent atelier on rue Laval.

Couture was a respected history and genre painter who had won medals at the Paris Salon for his work, but he taught his pupils to explore their own talent and ideas rather than the accepted academic norms. As other aspiring artists, in his spare time Manet copied the paintings of the great masters in the Louvre. Couture also encouraged him to journey around Europe to see the works of foreign masters such as Goya, Frans Hals, and Velázquez.

After six years of studying with Couture, Manet left his atelier in 1856 and, unconstrained by any financial difficulties, opened his own studio with his painter friend, Albert de Balleroy, in the rue Lavoisier. The following year Manet met Henri Fantin-Latour for the first time at the Louvre and they became great friends. Tragedy struck in 1859 when Manet returned to the studio to find their young assistant and occasional model, Alexandre, had hanged himself in the studio. Manet had the disturbing task of cutting him down and then telling his parents of the suicide. The business badly affected him and his friends; Charles Baudelaire wrote the poem *La Corde* (*The Rope*) about the incident.

Manet's first important painting, *The Absinthe Drinker*, revealed him taking his own artistic direction for the first time. He submitted it to the Salon but it was rejected despite the support of Eugène Delacroix. Around this time he met Edgar Degas and moved to a new studio on rue de la Victoire where he stayed for a year before moving to rue Guyot.

For the 1861 Salon, Manet submitted and had accepted two paintings, *The Spanish Singer* and a portrait of his parents, *Portrait of M. and Mme. Manet.* The former was well received and hung in a prominent position even though it was painted in a loose and unconventional style, completely unlike the other paintings surrounding it. *The Spanish Singer* was awarded an honorable mention. The latter painting became imbued with a poignant significance because his father died the following year.

All Manet's friends were similarly progressive thinkers who were passionate in their belief that art should reflect life as it was lived and not idealized historical fiction. His next work, *Music in the Tuileries*, was distinctly inspired by Velázquez and Frans Hals and included portraits of his friends Henri Fantin-Latour, Théophile Gautier, Charles Baudelaire, and others, as well as his brother, Eugène, and a self-portrait.

Together with Alfred Cadart and Felix Chevalier, Manet formed the Société des Aquafortistes in 1862 to produce and promote limited edition etchings. Through such endeavors Manet is credited with helping to revive the art of etching, something that had languished for years. Inevitably Manet discarded traditional etching techniques in order to explore different moods and approaches by way of shading and contrast through varied hatchings and linework. Also around this time Manet met the woman who was to become his most famous and favorite model, Victorine Meurent; he asked her to pose for him for *The Street Singer.*

In May 1863 Manet submitted *Le Bain*, better known today as *Le Déjeuner sur l'Herbe*, along with five other paintings to the Paris Salon. They rejected it for its scandalous content as much as for the way he painted the scene in bold blocks of color without conventional subtle shading transitions. He was not the only artist who was rejected and together the loud protests of the entire group of outcasts were heard by Emperor Louis-Napoleon who ordered the creation of the Salon des Refusés for works that were "quite as good as the pictures which had been accepted." When the exhibition opened in May, Manet showed three paintings–one of which was *Le Déjeuner sur l'Herbe*–and three etchings. The exhibition proved to be the beginning of the Impressionists.

Although *Le Déjeuner sur l'Herbe* was composed in classical fashion, the execution of the painting, which showed conventionally clothed men casually conversing with a naked woman in a park, proved scandalous. The models were Victorine Meurent as the nude lady, his brother Gustave, and his future brother-in-law Ferdinand Leenhoff. Manet wanted to subvert a conventional classical composition–such as Giorgione, Titian, and Courbet produced–and update it, but his critics completely missed the point, dismissing his interpretation as vulgar and unartistic.

Manet was deeply upset by the criticism and plunged into a deep bout of depression. Although he wanted to show in the conventional Salon, he also wanted to be modern to be true to himself; being rejected was a severe blow to his ego. He complained to Baudelaire, "Insults pour down on me like hail," to which Baudelaire pragmatically replied, "Do you think you are the first man put in this predicament?" but went on to reassure him that his genius would one day be recognized.

In 1863 Manet was challenged to paint a nude to hang in the Salon. He produced *Olympia*. Again using Victorine Meurent as his model, he based the composition of a reclining prostitute on the *Venus of Urbino* by Titian. She is shown as an unembarrassed odalisque calmly looking out at the viewer while her black slave presents her with a bouquet of white roses. Various elements in the work allude to her profession as a high-class prostitute, including the black cat, which at the time was a symbol of the profession (in Titian's similar painting the animal is a dog, the epitome of fidelity). It took two years for Manet to submit *Olympia* and when he did, to the surprise of many, the Salon accepted the painting and hung it in the 1865 exhibition.

Predictably, many critics were scandalized at the brazen nature of the work and the flat and loose way Manet had applied the paint. *Olympia* was described as vulgar and immoral, but other more perceptive viewers, such as Emile Zola, applauded it. The female nude, often Venus or Eve, is a well-known subject of artists, but she is usually depicted as being asleep or hesitant and coy about her nakedness. Manet did not follow this pattern and portrayed her instead as flagrant. One critic, Paul de Saint-Victor, described it as "art that has sunk so low it is not worthy of our censure." Some viewers apparently wanted to literally attack the painting. Antonin Proust remarked that "only the precautions taken by the administration prevented the painting being punctured and torn." Once again Manet found himself the object of popular scorn; his painting was lampooned in the press, but many of his contemporaries, such as Cézanne, Monet, and Courbet, openly praised it. His friend, Baudelaire, felt his friend, Manet, courted controversy but Manet disagreed and wrote to him, "They are raining insults down on me, I've never been led such a dance."

Hypocrisy was at the heart of much of the criticism of *Olympia*. Many wealthy Parisian men discreetly visited such women who lived in the shadows of society. They did not want their wives to be presented with such blatant evidence of their infidelities, let alone such a glamorous, exotic example as the subject of *Olympia*. For Manet, *Olympia* was "the first nude to represent modern reality."

By 1864 Manet was living at 34 rue des Batignolles with his studio in nearby rue Guyot. Like many of his friends he lived a bohemian lifestyle. He and Suzanne had married in the Netherlands on October 28, a year after his father died. His main theme now was the café society that surrounded him. He had become the acknowledged leader of the Parisian *avant garde* who met every Thursday at the Café Guerbois (also on rue des Batignolles), where all the most exciting artists and writers congregated to drink, argue, and carouse. They were dubbed the Batignolles Group and usually comprised Manet, Renoir, Sisley, Fantin-Latour, Zola, Frédéric Bazille, Louis Edmond Duranty, Degas, and Monet, plus occasional members, Paul Cézanne and Camille Pissarro.

The 1866 Salon rejected Manet's submission of *The Tragic Actor* and *The Fife Player*. One of his many supporters, Emile Zola, supported him in print with "A New Style in Painting: M. Edouard Manet," an article published in *L'Artiste: Revue de XIXe siècle*. Manet responded with a portrait of Emile Zola the following year, and it was accepted by the Salon for exhibition in 1868.

Manet was lucky enough to have inherited money so was not on the breadline like many of his contemporaries. After he had been rejected by the International Exhibition in 1867, he set up and paid for his own show in a tented pavillion outside the Universal Exhibition near the Pont de l'Alma. His mother worried that he was wasting his inheritance, whereas his friend Zola wrote a very supportive piece for *L'Evenment* and was fired as a consequence.

On a visit to London in summer 1868, Manet was introduced to Berthe Morisot by Fantin-Latour. They hit it off immediately, and although a respected artist herself, she agreed to pose for him for the painting, *The Balcony*, that fall. They remained close. Manet said of her, "This woman's work is exceptional. Too bad she's not a man." Berthe Morisot is credited with encouraging Manet

A Study for “A Bar at the Folies-Bergeres” *painted in 1881.* A Bar at the Folies-Bergeres *is probably one of Manet’s most recognizable paintings.*

to paint en plein air, which she herself customarily did. They critiqued each other's work and discussed and swapped painting techniques. In 1873 his portrait of her, *The Repose,* was hung at the Salon. Their relationship was formalized in 1874 when she became his sister-in-law upon marrying Eugène Manet.

In July 1870 the Franco-Prussian War broke out and, following the establishment of the unstable Third Republic, Manet closed his studio and stored his paintings with the art collector Théodore Duret. It was a very good decision because his studio was destroyed during the conflict. He remained in Paris but sent his family away to safety in the Pyrenees. In November 1870 he joined the Garde Nationale. But within three months he joined his family in Arçachon. After the Communards' revolution in May he returned to Paris where life slowly returned to normal.

The new meeting place for the avant-garde was Nouvelle Athènes on Place Pigalle. After the destruction of his old studie, Manet was forced to find a new one and in July 1872 moved to 4 rue de Saint-Pétersbourg.

In 1874 Manet was invited to exhibit at the first Impressionist exhibition, but he refused. Despite his love for modernism and the abuse he had endured because of it at the hands of the Salon, he was still an ardent supporter of the Salon and wanted and needed such establishment approval for his work. Even so, the Salon refused to hang two of his paintings that season (*The Swallows* and *Masked Ball at the Opera*), but accepted a third work, *The Railway.*

Manet decided to open his studio to the public so they could see for themselves the rejected paintings, as well as *The Artist* and *The Laundress* and other works. Over 4,000 people came to see his private exhibition. The following year the Salon relented and accepted *Faure as Hamlet,* but rejected *Nana,* an informal portrait of a young prostitute in her underclothes standing beside an obviously wealthy client. The model was a well-known grande coquette, Henriette Hauser, the Parisian mistress of the Prince of Orange. Determined to show the painting to the public, Manet managed to hang *Nana* in the window of Giroux's luxury boutique on the Boulevard des Capucines where it almost caused a riot.

Manet declined to offer any paintings to the Salon the following year. This may have been pride but also expediency as his health was beginning to trouble him; he didn't even hold his own private exhibition.

In 1878 the Manet family moved to 39 rue de Saint-Petersburg and the following year Manet took what proved to be his last studio at 77 rue d'Amsterdam. By the fall his left leg was giving him trouble and he took treatment at Bellevue, but his leg became worse and his general health suffered. In 1880 a rapprochement of sorts was reached with the Salon when it accepted his work and awarded him a second place medal for *M. Pertuiset, the Lion-Hunter*, which gave Manet *hors concours* status meaning that he could exhibit unchallenged from then on. Ironically, it was by no means one of his better paintings, being almost primitive in style and execution. Nevertheless he had become almost an establishment figure and on December 30, 1881, his stature was confirmed when he was made a Chevalier de la Légion d'Honneur.

Despite his failing health, Manet still had one great painting left in him. *A Bar at the Folies-Bergère* was hung at the Salon in 1882 and yet again proved controversial, this time for his depiction of a woman working in the notorious Folies-Bergère, a cabaret-cum-brothel and meeting place where no respectable person would wish to be seen, although Manet himself was a frequent visitor, sketching the scenes around him. Having decided on his subject, he invited a young woman called Suzon who worked there to pose for him. He set up a bar in his studio and asked her to pose in her work uniform.

The painting was critically well received but many viewers again perceived his principal subject as a prostitute (as barmaids at the Folies-Bergère were widely believed to be) who flouted conventional society. By this time Manet's output was very restricted; he was too incapacitated during his last months to visit his studio. He had to paint at home and ultimately from his sickbed. Despite treatment, the condition of his left leg deteriorated and on April 20, 1883, it was amputated. Ten days later, on April 30, Edouard Manet died, aged 51. The cause of death was probably tertiary syphilis.

Manet left his entire estate to Suzanne on condition that she in turn leave everything to Léon, a tacit confirmation that he was, indeed, his father. He was buried at Passy Cemetery. His pall bearers were Claude Monet, Antonin Proust, Emile Zola, Théodore Duret, Henri Fantin-Latour, Alfred Stevens, and Philippe Burty. The following year a retrospective of his works was held at the École des Beaux-Arts. In 1890, Claude Monet organized a public subscription to raise funds to buy *Olympia* for the French nation.

WOMAN WITH A JUG

1858–60, Ordrupgaard, Copenhagen
61 x 54.5 cm

THE ABSINTHE DRINKER

1859, Ny Carlsberg Glyptotek, Copenhagen
No dimensions given

Plate 3

PORTRAIT OF MONSIEUR AND MADAME AUGUSTE MANET

1860, Musée d'Orsay, Paris

110 x 90 cm

THE SPANISH SINGER

1860, Metropolitan Museum of Art, New York City
147.3 x 114.3 cm

Plate 5

THE SHIP'S DECK

1860, National Gallery of Victoria, Melbourne, Australia
56.4 x 47 cm

THE SURPRISED NYMPH

1859–61, Museu Nacional de Bellas Artes, Buenos Aires, Argentina
146 x 114.3 cm

BOY WITH A SWORD

1861, Metropolitan Museum of Art, New York City
131.1 x 93.4 cm

LADY WITH A FAN (BAUDELAIRE'S MISTRESS RECLINING)

Plate 8

1862, Museum of Fine Arts, Budapest
89.5 x 113 cm

Plate 9

LOLA DE VALENCE

1862, Musée d'Orsay, Paris

123 x 92 cm

MADEMOISELLE V . . . IN THE COSTUME OF AN ESPADA

1862, Metropolitan Museum of Art, New York City

165.1 x 127.6 cm

MUSIC IN THE TUILERIES GARDENS

1862, National Gallery, London

76.2 x 118.1 cm

THE OLD MUSICIAN

1862, National Gallery of Art, Washington, DC
187.4 x 248.2 cm

Plate 13

OYSTERS

1862, National Gallery of Art, Washington, DC
39.2 x 46.8 cm

STREET SINGER

c. 1862, Museum of Fine Arts Boston

171.1 x 105.8 cm

Plate 15

VICTORINE MEURENT

c. 1862, Musuem of Fine Arts Boston

42.9 x 43.8 cm

YOUNG WOMAN RECLINING IN SPANISH COSTUME

1862–63, Yale University Art Gallery, New Haven, Connecticut
94.7 x 113.7 cm

Plate 17

FISHING

1862–63, Metropolitan Museum of Art, New York City
76.8 x 123.2 cm

LUNCHEON ON THE GRASS (LE DÉJEUNER SUR L'HERBE)

1863, Musée d'Orsay, Paris

208 x 264.5 cm

OLYMPIA

1863, Musée d'Orsay, Paris
130 x 190 cm

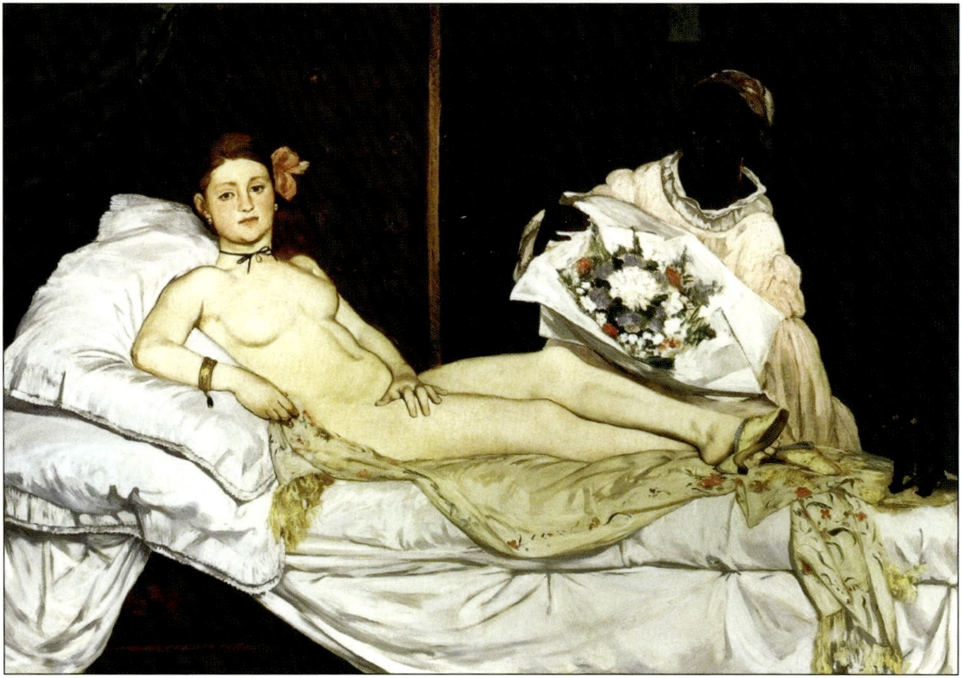

YOUNG MAN IN THE COSTUME OF A MAJO

1863, Metropolitan Museum of Art, New York City

188 x 124.8 cm

Plate 21

BASKET OF FRUIT

c. 1864, Museum of Fine Arts Boston
37.8 x 44.4 cm

THE BATTLE OF THE U.S.S. "KEARSARGE" AND THE C.S.S. "ALABAMA"

Plate 22

1864, Philadelphia Museum of Art
137.8 x 128.9 cm

THE DEAD CHRIST WITH ANGELS

1864, Metropolitan Museum of Art, New York City

179.4 x 149.9 cm

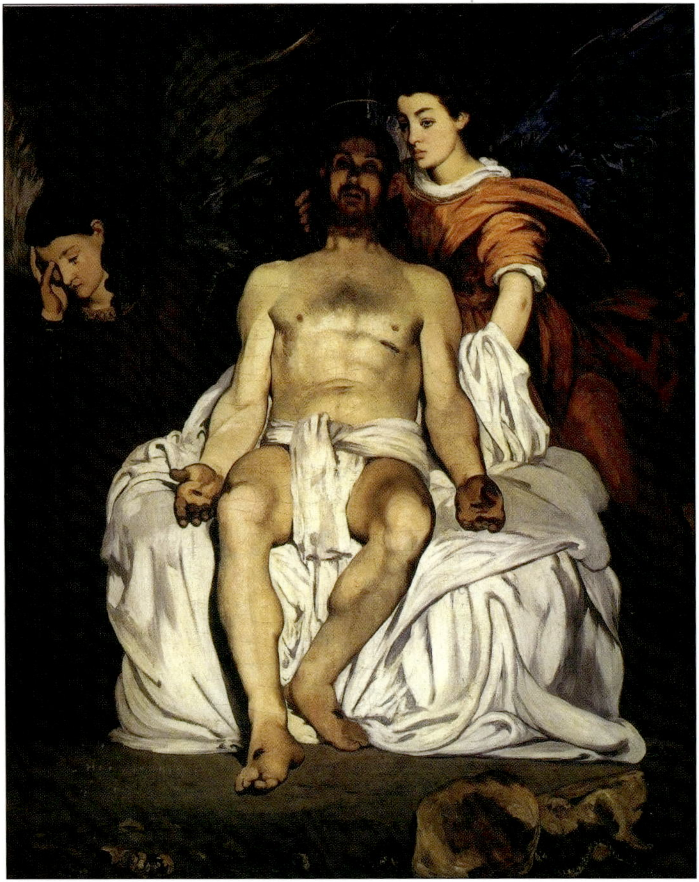

THE "KEARSARGE" AT BOULOGNE

1864, Metropolitan Museum of Art, New York City
81.6 x 100 cm

Plate 25

VASE OF PEONIES ON A PEDESTAL

1864, Musée d'Orsay, Paris

93.2 x 70.2 cm

FISH (STILL LIFE)

1864, Art Institute of Chicago
73.4 x 92.1 cm

Plate 27

THE DEAD TOREADOR

1865, National Gallery of Art, Washington, DC
75.9 x 153.3 cm

THE BULLFIGHT

1865–66, Art Institute of Chicago

48 x 60.4 cm

Plate 29

JESUS MOCKED BY THE SOLDIERS

1865, Art Institute of Chicago

190.8 x 148.3 cm

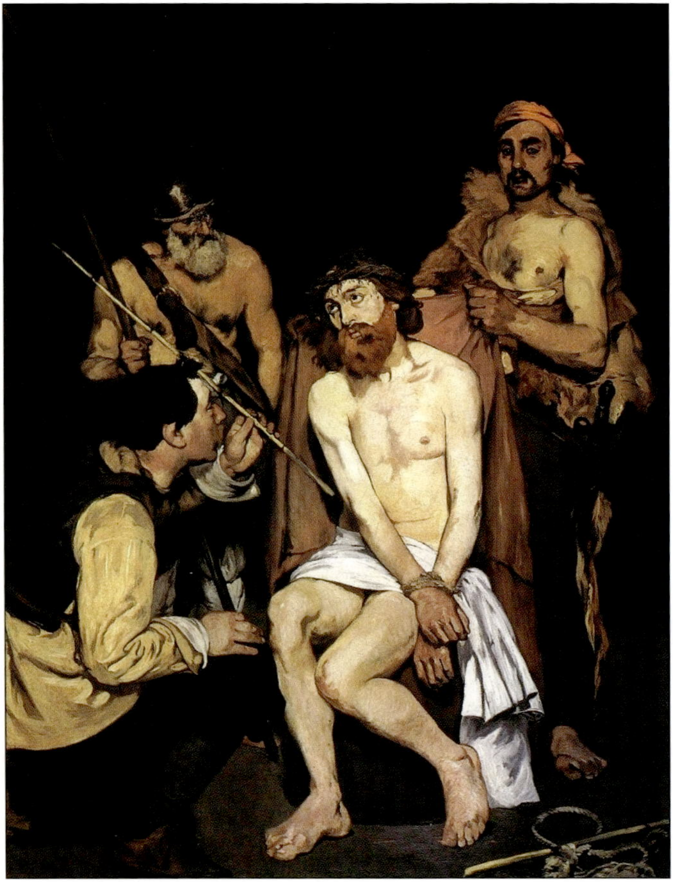

MONK AT PRAYER

1865, Museum of Fine Arts Boston

146.4 x 115 cm

THE RACES AT LONGCHAMP

1866, Art Institute of Chicago

43.9 x 84.5 cm

WOMEN AT THE RACES

1866, Cincinnati Art Museum, Ohio

42.2 x 32.1 cm

THE FIFE PLAYER

1866, Musée d'Orsay, Paris

161 x 97 cm

A MATADOR

1866–67, Metropolitan Museum of Art, New York City

171.1 x 113 cm

STILL LIFE WITH MELON AND PEACHES

1866, National Gallery of Art, Washington, DC

68.3 x 91 cm

BEGGAR WITH OYSTERS (PHILOSOPHER)

1865–67, Art Institute of Chicago

187.3 x 108 cm

Plate 37

YOUNG LADY IN 1866

1866, Metropolitan Museum of Art, New York City

185.1 x 128.6 cm

THE TRAGIC ACTOR (ROUVIÈRE AS HAMLET)

1866, National Gallery of Art, Washington, DC
187.2 x 108.1 cm

Plate 39

EXECUTION OF THE EMPEROR MAXIMILIAN

1867, Museum of Fine Arts Boston

195.9 x 259.7 cm

THE EXECUTION OF EMPEROR MAXIMILIAN

1867–68, Ny Carlsberg Glyptotek, Copenhagen

252 x 305 cm

THE FUNERAL

1867, Metropolitan Museum of Art, New York City
72.7 x 90.5 cm

THE LUNCHEON

1868, Bayerische Staatsgemaldesammlungen–Neue Pinakothek, Munich
118 x 154 cm

EMILE ZOLA

1868, Musée d'Orsay, Paris

146.5 x 114 cm

THE BALCONY

1868–69, Musée d'Orsay, Paris

170 x 124.5 cm

MOONLIGHT, BOULOGNE

1868, Musée d'Orsay, Paris

81.92 x 100.97 cm

ON THE BEACH AT BOULOGNE

1868, Virginia Museum of Fine Arts, Richmond
No dimensions given

Plate 47

REPOSE: PORTRAIT OF BERTHE MORISOT

1870, Rhode Island School of Design Museum of Art

147.96 x 111.13 cm

EVA GONZALEZ

1870, National Gallery, London

191.1 x 133.4 cm

Plate 49

INTERIOR AT ARCACHON

1871, Sterling and Francine Clark Art Institute, Williamstown, Massachusetts
39.4 x 53.7 cm

Plate 50

BERTHE MORISOT WITH A BOUQUET OF VIOLETS

1872, Musée d'Orsay, Paris

55 x 39 cm

MASKED BALL AT THE OPERA

1873, National Gallery of Art, Washington, DC

59.7 x 73 cm

ON THE BEACH

1873, Musée d'Orsay, Paris
95.9 x 73 cm

Plate 53

THE RAILWAY

1873, National Gallery of Art, Washington, DC
93.3 x 111.5 cm

THE SWALLOWS

1873, E.G. Bührle Collection, Zurich
65 x 81 cm

Plate 55

LADY WITH FANS

1873, Musée d'Orsay, Paris
113 x 165.7 cm

READING

Between 1848 and 1883, Musée d'Orsay, Paris
61 x 75.2 cm

Plate 57

ARGENTEUIL

1874, Musée des Beaux-Arts de Tournai, Belgium
151.77 x 114.94 cm

BOATING

1874, Metropolitan Museum of Art, New York City
97.2 x 130.2 cm

Plate 59

THE MONET FAMILY IN THEIR GARDEN AT ARGENTEUIL

1874, Metropolitan Museum of Art, New York City

61 x 99.7 cm

BANKS OF THE SEINE AT ARGENTEUIL

1874, The Courtauld Gallery, London

62.3 x 103 cm

Plate 61

THE GRAND CANAL, VENICE (BLUE VENICE)

1875, Shelburne Museum, Shelburne, Vermont

58.74 x 71.44 cm

STÉPHANE MALLARMÉ

1876, Musée d'Orsay, Paris
26.99 x 35.88 cm

Plate 63

BEFORE THE MIRROR

1876, Solomon R. Guggenheim Museum, New York City

92.1 × 71.4 cm

FAURE AS HAMLET

1876–77, Hamburger Kunsthalle, Germany
No dimensions given

Plate 65

NANA

1877, Hamburger Kunsthalle, Germany

154.31 x 114.94 cm

PLUM BRANDY

1878, National Gallery of Art, Washington, DC
73.6 x 50.2 cm

Plate 67

THE CAFE-CONCERT

1879, The Walters Art Museum, Baltimore, Maryland

47.3 x 39.1 cm

CHEZ LE PERE LATHUILLE

1879, Musée des Beaux-Arts de Tournai, Belgium
No dimensions given

Plate 69

WOMAN FASTENING HER GARTER

1878–79, Ordrupgaard, Copenhagen

55 x 46 cm

GEORGE MOORE

1879, Metropolitan Museum of Art, New York City
55.2 x 35.2 cm

Plate 71

WOMAN READING

1879–80, Art Institute of Chicago

61.2 x 50.7 cm

ANTONIN PROUST

1880, Toledo Museum of Art, Ohio

129.5 x 95.9 cm

Plate 73

MADAME MANET AT BELLEVUE

1880, Metropolitan Museum of Art, New York City

80.6 x 60.3 cm

WOMAN WITH A CAT

c. 1880, Tate Britain, London
92.1 x 73 cm

Plate 75

MADEMOISELLE ISABELLE LEMONNIER

1879–82, Metropolitan Museum of Art, New York City

55.9 x 46.4 cm

CLEMENCEAU

1879–80, Musee d'Orsay, Paris
94.5 x 74 cm

Plate 77

AT THE MILLINER'S

1881, Fine Arts Museums of San Francisco, de Young

85 x 73.7 cm

AUTUMN

1881, Musee des Beaux-Arts de Nancy, France

73 x 50.8 cm

Plate 79

FLOWERS IN A CRYSTAL VASE

c. 1882, National Gallery of Art, Washington, DC
32.7 x 24.5 cm

Plate 80

A BAR AT THE FOLIES-BERGERE

1881–82, The Courtauld Gallery, London

96 x 130 cm

Plate 81

PINKS AND CLEMATIS IN A CRYSTAL VASE

1882, Musée d'Orsay, Paris

56 x 35.5 cm

THE HOUSE AT RUEIL

1882, National Gallery of Victoria, Melbourne, Australia

92.8 x 73.5 cm

INDEX